Spiritual Thoughts for Today's Teacher

✠

Timothy J. McMullen

Published by

Prospect Hill Company

61 Prospect Street

Brockton, MA 02301

1-800-586-1951

508-583-2072

Fax: 508-587-8248

ISBN 0-9664050-1-3

Copyright © 1998 Timothy J. McMullen

Dedication

❧❧

*To all those teachers
who have dedicated their
time and talents
to educate our youth.*

❧❧

Godspeed.

*"I praise you, so wonderfully
you made me;
wonderful are your works!"*

—Psalm 139:14

*L*ord Jesus, let me show my students how wonderful Your great and vast works are. Teach me ways to illustrate that even Your "little works" such as snowflakes, a big smile, a cozy fire, autumn leaves should be appreciated each and every day.

Amen.

*"As every thread of gold
is valuable, so is every
moment of time."*

—John Manson

As a teacher, my time with my students is so limited, Lord. Help me utilize every precious minute and focus on the lesson at hand.

Amen.

*"What a man thinks in his heart
is what he becomes."*

—Conventional Wisdom

*T*each us, Lord, that good thoughts bring forth great actions. Those great actions may not seem so great but anything coming from the heart is a true sign of our love.

Amen.

"He who has no fire in himself cannot warm others."

—Unknown

Holy Spirit, enkindle in my heart a love like no other for being a teacher. Let me start each class refreshed with Your love and let my enthusiasm shine throughout my classroom. Give me peace of mind that I know the lesson and will teach it well.

Amen.

"Is prayer your steering wheel or your spare tire?"

—Carrie ten Boom

*S*o many use prayer as their emergency vehicle when they are desperate. Lord, show me the way to teach my students daily prayer. I know once they find the peace and consolation of daily prayer, they will use it to steer their lives in a positive manner towards You.

Amen.

"God looked at everything
he had made, and he
found it very good."

—Genesis 1:31

*G*od doesn't make junk! Assure all of my students that each and every one of us was put on this earth for a reason. We owe it to ourselves and to You, Lord, to do the best that we can!

Amen.

"Life is not as short but that there is always time enough for courtesy."

—Ralph Waldo Emerson

*I*t seems in this modern age of ours, courtesy is a thing of the past. Lord Jesus, show me how to teach my students respect and courtesy for our elderly, our superiors, our parents and our peers.

Amen.

"Grant me the courage not to give up even though I think it is hopeless."

—Chester W. Nimitz

O Holy Spirit, my students need to be taught the importance of one of your seven gifts ... courage. Consistently give them the courage that they need and make hopeless a word that does not exist in their vocabulary.

Amen.

"Walk your talk."

—Native American Proverb

*D*ear Lord, let me be strong and express my feelings about You and Your commandments. Allow others to see that what I say, I do. Let me be a walking, talking example of Your Love.

Amen.

"May you live all the days
of your life."

—Conventional Wisdom

*L*ife is so precious, Lord Jesus. Remind me daily that I was sent here by You and let me fulfill the purpose You have for me. To appreciate all the goodness You have created, I owe it to You and to myself to truly "live" each day of my life.

Amen.

"Whether you think you can or think you can't, you're right."

—Henry Ford

*P*ositive attitude is so valuable in these young peoples' lives. Let me instill the importance of waking up each day with an upbeat outlook on life. O most Holy Spirit, be my guide.

Amen.

"The past cannot be changed, the future is still in your grasp."

—Conventional Wisdom

*G*uide me, Lord, to teach my students to begin each day anew. You alone know what the future holds for us. You alone have given each of us the power within to release the past and to focus on the future.

Amen.

"Kind words produce kind actions and they cost no more than unkind words."

—Jeremy Bentham

*H*eavenly Father, may I emphasize to my students that being considerate and thoughtful cost them nothing but will reap huge dividends now and also in Your kingdom of heaven.

Amen.

*"Children are a great deal more apt
to follow your lead
than the way you point."*

—Conventional Wisdom

*Y*ou, Lord, are the true Light of the World. Enrich my students with a better understanding of Your ways. Guide me to Your light and lead my students to Your heavenly path.

Amen.

"I touch the future. I teach."

—Christa McAuliffe

*D*ear Lord, I have always wanted to affect the future. As a teacher, I finally have the chance. Let me help my students touch the stars, challenge their dreams and forever affect the way they look upon You.

Amen.

*"Grant that we may not so much
seek to be understood
as to understand."*

—St. Francis of Assisi

*G*od of Love, it is important that the lesson I teach be understood, but show me how to keep an open mind and an attentive ear for my students as well. By understanding and listening to my students I will be a better educator.

Amen.

"One today is worth two tomorrows; never leave that till tomorrow which you can do today."

—Benjamin Franklin

*G*od, I am the worst procrastinator. Help me realize how important it is to complete my tasks today and not take the easy way out and put it off till tomorrow.

Amen.

"The heights by great men
reached and kept
were not attained by sudden flight,
But they,
while their companions slept,
were toiling upward in the night."

—Henry Wadsworth Longfellow

*R*emind me, God, of this quote next time I am toiling over my curriculum and papers late into the night. I need to know that my "late nights" will pay off with my students because of a detailed, well thought out lesson.

Amen.

*"My son, if you receive my words
and treasure my commands, ...
Then you will understand the fear
of the LORD;
the knowledge of God
you will find;"*

—Proverbs 2:1,5

*W*hy would one fear You, Lord?
With the knowledge You have given me,
help me explain to my students this
difficult concept so they will understand
how All-Loving and All-Powerful You are.

Amen.

"The child is not there for you, but you are there for the child."

—Samuel Raphael Hirsch

*H*elp me understand my role as an educator, loving Jesus. Remind me when I begin to get on my "soap box" that my students are not here for me, I am here for them. Make me aware of opportunities to listen to their stories and to properly answer their questions.

Amen.

"Be cheerful.
Of all the things you wear
your expression is the
most important."

—Conventional Wisdom

*C*hrist Jesus, put a constant smile on my face to be an indication of the Light of Your Love and allow me to share it with my students. Keep in me a joyful heart and let it be contagious to my students.

Amen.

"Every problem contains the seeds to its own solution."

—Stanley Arnold

O Risen Christ, like the mustard seed that found a way to blossom in sand and rock, help me make my students realize that for every problem a solution can be found. With You, Lord, everything is attainable and every problem can be solved.

Amen.

"For we are his handiwork ..."

—Ephesians 2:10

*H*eavenly Father, my students need to know that bodies and minds are Your handiwork. With Your help I will be able to teach my class a respect of their bodies and an appreciation of their minds. Give me the wisdom to show them responsible ways of improving these gifts You have given us.

Amen.

"The art of teaching consists in helping students feel that although you may stand in front of them, you're really behind them."

*G*ive my students the knowledge of my concern for them. Let them feel confident that I can be trusted not only as a good teacher but as a friend – a friend who will care, listen and only give advice when asked.

Amen.

*"To teach a child's mind
a teacher must
capture his heart."*

—Haim G. Ginnott

*C*hrist Jesus, creativity is so important in my role as a teacher. Allow my creativity and sincerity to capture the imagination of my students. We can grow together in Your love if we take time to care about one another.

Amen.

*" 'LORD, if my brother sins against
me, how often must
I forgive him? As many as seven
times?' Jesus answered,
'I say to you, not seven times
but seventy-seven times.' "*

—Matthew 18:21-22

*F*ree me from holding a grudge, Almighty One. You have taught us through Your example on the cross how to forgive others. Allow me to forgive gracefully and with no remorse towards the offender.

Amen.

"The real secret of success is enthusiasm. When people get excited they make a success of their lives."

—Walter Chrysler

*F*ather, I love enthusiastic students! One of my goals that I have set for this class is to give my students a clear understanding of Your Word. Guide me to be successful at this task by being informative, interesting and inventive. I know that with Your help my students will get excited about Your teachings.

Amen.

"I can alter my life by altering my attitude."

—Unknown

*M*y attitude is an important factor in my life, Lord Jesus. Keep reminding me how significant it is in front of my classroom. Having a positive outlook is just not enough. Let me learn from Your example to have an attitude filled with love and understanding always.

Amen.

*"Could a greater miracle take place
than for us to look through each
other's eyes for an instant?"*

—Thoreau

*L*et me stop and think before I
pass judgement on my students. Allow
me to consider all the possibilities and for
a moment, let me see what the world looks
like through their eyes.

Amen.

"He came to what was his own, but his own people did not accept him."

—John I:11

*L*ord Jesus, sometimes we do not get the respect that we deserve from the people closest to us. I must teach my students to look beyond this disappointment and move on. I know that You are always there and Your acceptance is all they need.

Amen.

"You give but little when you give of your possessions.
It is when you give of yourself that you truly give."

—Kahlil Gibran

*R*enew the spirit of charity in each of us, Lord. Remind me that when I give a student my time, a sympathetic ear, a reassuring smile, or a congratulatory pat on the back, it means more to that individual because it comes from my heart.

Amen.

"Fear knocked at the door.
Faith answered.
No one was there."

—Old Gaelic Saying

*A*ll Loving Father, sometimes it is frightening to think of my duties as a teacher. Shaping the future of these young minds is a big responsibility. Let me have faith in You to know that I can teach Your Word and to show these students the right path.

Amen.

"Love cures people,
both the ones who give it
and the ones who receive it."

—Dr. Karl Menninger

*Y*our Love cures all, Lord. I feel my best when I share it with others. Enable me to spread it to my students so they can share it with everyone they meet.
Amen.

*"Plan your work – work
your plan."*

—Conventional Wisdom

Help me, Lord, to know that one needs more than just a plan. One needs to work and work hard to accomplish a goal. Give me the energy and enthusiasm to work my plan as best as I can.

Amen.

*"Years from now it will not
matter what kind of car
you drive, what size house
you lived in, or what size
your clothes were.
But the world may be a little better
because you were
important in the life of a child."*

—Anonymous

*F*ree me from being caught up in the material things of this world. Help me to forget about myself and concentrate on the students that You have put in my care. Through my words and example, let Your teachings be important to their future.

Amen.

"It's funny how from simple things, the best things begin."

—B. Streisand

*S*implicity is a word sometimes forgotten in this complicated world of ours. Let me teach about the simple things in life that You give us, Lord, and how a lot of times we treasure these simple things the most.

Amen.

"Have patience with all things, but chiefly have patience with yourself."

—St. Francis de Sales

*E*ncourage me to have patience with myself and to believe that I can accomplish the tasks at hand. Grant me patience with my students as well and provide them with encouragement along the way.

Amen.

"We are all pencils
in the hand of God."

—Mother Teresa

*A*lmighty God, give me the ability to be a good teacher. Use me, like a pencil, to erase the anxiety of my students' worries by illustrating Your Loving Word in each class.

Amen.

"If you treat an individual as if he were what he ought to be and could be, he will become what he ought to be and could be."

—Goethe

*A*llow me to show respect to my students, Lord Jesus. I want to be quick to offer praise and highlight the good qualities of my students. Permit them to realize that they can be all they want to be.

Amen.

*"Imagination is not
just a child's place."*

—T. J. Flaherty

*A*ssist me to use my imagination to make my lesson plan more interesting and fun. Let imagination be a big part of my classroom. Allow me to use my words and actions as a paintbrush and paint them a beautiful picture of Your plan for us.

Amen.

*"The real purpose of
our existence is not to make
a living — but to make a life,
a worthy, whole and useful life."*

—Conventional Wisdom

Sometimes, Lord, we get caught up in the hustle and bustle of making ends meet. Help me realize that our purpose is not to exist day to day but to really *live* each day and make a difference. Let me show my students, by Your example, that they too can make a difference in this wonderful world of Yours.

Amen.

"The light of God surrounds me,
The love of God enfolds me,
The power of God protects me,
The presence of God watches
over me,
Whatever I am, God is."

—Prayer Card

*L*ord, show my students that Your "light" and "love" give us endless opportunities. Let me remind them that You are always present and we will forever be protected by Your watchful care.

Amen.

" 'I have many flowers,' he said, 'but the children are the most beautiful flowers of all.' "

—Oscar Wilde

Children are like flowers; they both need constant care and weeding. Let me help my students sort out the "weeds" that are out there and show them how to become spiritually strong so they can grow into beautiful adults.

Amen.

"The only way to multiply happiness is to divide it up."

—Conventional Wisdom

God, You have given us unlimited resources to find happiness. Let me channel into this reservoir and spread Your Good News to my students. True happiness is meant to be shared.

Amen.

*"All problems become smaller
if you don't dodge them
but confront them."*

—Unknown

*L*ord, when it comes to problems that my students have, let me focus on them immediately. Give me an attentive ear and help resolve the issue before it escalates into a bigger problem.

Amen.

*"The potential possibilities
of any child are the most intriguing
and stimulating
in all creation."*

—Ray L. Wilbur

*L*ord, the possibilities for Your children are overwhelming. Let my students grasp at these moments and use them to the best of their ability.

Amen.

"I raise my eyes toward the mountains.
From where will my help come?
My help comes from the LORD,
the maker of heaven and earth."

—Psalm 121:1-2

*L*ord, creator of heaven and earth, remind me that You will be with me today, tomorrow and forever. All I have to do is ask and it will be given to me, seek and I shall find, knock and You will open the door for me.

Amen.

"JOY"

"*Jesus first,*
Others second,
Yourself last."

—Unknown

Heavenly Father, teach these young people the joy of putting You first, others second and themselves last. When they have experienced this "Joy" they will delight and rejoice in Your everlasting peace.

Amen.

*"Every individual's work is a
portrait of oneself."*

—Conventional Wisdom

*C*reator of heaven and earth,
You strived for perfection when you
created us, Your children. In everything
they do, let my students strive for
perfection. Help them realize that their
efforts will always be a signature of
themselves.

Amen.

"Most people don't plan to fail;
they fail to plan."

—John L. Beckley

*D*ear Jesus, planning is essential, not only in teaching but life in general. I want to teach my students that You should always be a big part of their plan. If they consistently include You in their plans, they will always reach their goals.

Amen.

"A load of books does not equal one teacher."

—Chinese Proverb

*L*ord, it is an awesome responsibility to be a teacher. Show my students how You affect our daily lives. Help me use my life as a real example of Your mercies and wonder. Allow me to teach them what textbooks cannot.

Amen.

"All of the flowers of all of the tomorrows are in the seeds of today."

—Conventional Wisdom

*Y*ou, O Lord, will make everything flower at its appropriate time. Use me today as a gardener to cultivate these students. Make sure I instruct them correctly, helping them blossom into their full potential.

Amen.

"WWJD"

"What Would Jesus Do?"

—Unknown

*C*an you imagine if these students prefaced each decision they made with these four words? At this age, my students make so many decisions; let these four words guide them to choose the correct ones.

Amen.

"Students have the energy, imagination and intelligence to make a difference in their community. They need only be asked to show what they can do."

—Kathleen Kennedy Townsend

*L*ord, in my role as teacher, You allow me to give back to my community. Thank You! Help me come up with creative ways to show my students how they can contribute and share their young talents.

Amen.

"The way to be happy
is to make others happy."

—Conventional Wisdom

*L*ord, there is no greater joy than making others happy. Having an occasional laugh with my students and still maintaining their respect is the hallmark of a healthy classroom.

Amen.

"Then he sat down, called the Twelve, and said to them, 'If any one wishes to be first, he shall be the last of all and the servant of all'."

—Mark 9:35

*O*God, let me point out to my students the beautiful, loving, unselfish ways of Your disciple, Mother Teresa. She indeed was a modern day example of Your humility. Mother Teresa clearly illustrated that by serving others, we put ourselves last and we put You, Jesus, first.

Amen.

"No difficulties, no discovery;
no pains, no gains."

—Unknown

*L*ord, Your world can be so exciting when one takes chances and dares to do what they dream about. Allow my students to empower themselves and discover how new experiences can be so rewarding. If they fail, let me be there so we can dust off and try again together.

Amen.

"The best portion of an individual's life is the little, nameless, unremembered acts of kindness and love."

—William Wordsworth

*Y*our "Little Flower," Saint Theresa of Lisieux, taught us about "little things" and ways of doing the smallest things with love. Please make me aware of the opportunities that present themselves each day to do an act of kindness for someone.

Amen.

*"I am to be so busy today
that I must spend more time than
usual in prayer."*

—Conventional Wisdom

*W*e all know the nutritional rewards of starting the day with a good breakfast. Show my students the spiritual rewards and the benefits that are received by starting each day in prayer to You, Jesus, especially on those days that are so busy.

Amen.

"Let nothing disturb you,
let nothing frighten you:
everything passes away
except God;
God alone is sufficient."

—St. Theresa of Lisieux

*T*his modern world of ours is sometimes scary, Lord. Help me teach my students that if they believe in You, nothing will frighten or disturb them and that You and You alone are everything.

Amen.

"If you want to put the world right, start with yourself."

—Conventional Wisdom

*S*ome days I feel that I can save the world, Lord. I have so many great ideas. Give me courage to right the wrongs, the strength to keep trying and faith in only You.

Amen.

"Puzzled about life ... pray."

—T.J. Flaherty

*S*aving God, when I can't make sense of things and life appears as a puzzle, give me faith and show me where all the "pieces" go. When my students are puzzled, give me the right words to show them that with You in their lives, the puzzle will be complete.

Amen.

"The God of peace be with all of you. Amen."

—Romans 15:33

*W*hat a wonderful blessing one can bestow upon anyone! Bless my students, Father, with Your peace throughout this school year and forever.

Amen.

"The big question is whether you are going to be able to say a hearty yes to your adventure."

—Joseph Campbell

*L*ord, grant that every day be an adventure in my classroom. Allow me to embrace each day with a hearty "Yes" and let my enthusiasm envelop my students' interests and encourage their quest for knowledge of You.

Amen.

*"Give me a sense of
humor, Lord;
Give me the grace to see a joke,
To get some happiness from life,
And pass it on to other folk."*

—Saying on a Prayer Card

*S*ometimes I get too serious in front of my class, Lord. Lighten me up and allow me a sense of humor with my students. Remind me that a joyful heart creates a long and healthy life.

Amen.

"What this world needs is
fewer rules and more
good examples."

—Conventional Wisdom

*T*ime and time again, You have proven to us, Lord, children learn what they live. I pray that I set a good example to this younger generation. May they see the examples that You have set through my daily actions.

Amen.

"Obstacles are those frightful things you see when you take your eyes off your goal."

—Henry Ford

*M*y goal in this class, Lord Jesus, is to reach out to each student and share Your great love with them as You have shared Your love with me. My goal is lofty, Lord, so do not let me worry about the obstacles I will incur.

Amen.

*"Therefore, do not throw away
your confidence; it will have
great recompense."*

—Hebrews 10:35

Heavenly Father, let me
strengthen in my students the confidence
that they should have in themselves. Help
me show them that believing in oneself
reaps great rewards. It is only when they
believe and love themselves that they
truly can believe in and love others.

Amen.

"An admission of error is a sign of strength rather than a confession of weakness."

—Conventional Wisdom

*L*ord, lead me in all that I do and when I make a mistake with my students, let me be quick to acknowledge it. The knowledge of your strength is my security and I realize that everyone makes mistakes, but only the strong admit to them.

Amen.

"Whatever you do, put romance and enthusiasm into the life of our children."

—Margaret Ramsey MacDonald

*L*ord, romance can be about many things. My love for You and Your children have made me a teacher. Let this love be translated for my students as romance and enthusiasm for all of the beauty in Your world.

Amen.

*"Do the very best
you possibly can ...
And then leave the
outcome to God."*

—Conventional Wisdom

*M*ake me a good teacher,
O Lord. I can do my best by carefully
planning my lessons, listening intently to
my students and giving glory to You in
each of my classes. When I have done all
that I can may I be comforted by leaving
the rest in Your good hands.

Amen.

*"Kids may forget
what you said ... but they'll never
forget how
you made them feel."*

—Carl W. Buehner

*U*nique and Special, that is how I want my students to feel after they leave my classroom. Heavenly Creator, you made each and every one of us different, making sure we were unique in many ways. Allow me to show my students what a marvelous gift You have given us.

Amen.

*"For God commands the angels
to guard you in all your ways."*

—Psalm 91:11

*G*uardian of All Life, nuture a respect in my students for their guardian angels and show them how important these angels are to all of us. Remind me that I should pray to my guardian angel for guidance in teaching.

Amen.

*"If at first you don't succeed,
try, try again."*

—William E. Hickson

*H*elp me realize, Lord, that if we learn from our failures, we have already experienced a bit of success. I hope never to give up on my students. Give me strength to find the way to get through, even to the toughest of students.

Amen.

*"To handle yourself,
use your head; to handle others, use
your heart."*

—Conventional Wisdom

*O*Most Holy Spirit, let me find the right mixture of love and logic in dealing with all situations. When You present difficulties for me to handle, allow me to use this mixture to change these difficulties into opportunities.

Amen.

SEPTEMBER – 1998

Sunday	Monday	Tuesday	Wednesday	Thursday	Friday	Saturday
		1	2	3 St. Gregory the Great	4	5
6 23rd Sunday in Ordinary Time	7 Labor Day	8 Birth of the Virgin Mary	9 St. Peter Claver	10	11	12
13 24th Sunday in Ordinary Time	14 The Holy Cross	15 Our Lady of Sorrows	16 St. Cornelius	17 St. Robert Bellarmine	18	19 St. Januarius
20 25th Sunday in Ordinary Time	21 St. Matthew the Apostle	22	23	24	25	26 Ss. Cosmas and Damian
27 26th Sunday in Ordinary Time	28 St. Wenceslaus	29 Ss. Michael, Gabriel, and Raphael	30 St. Jerome			